The GEEK Baby Book

A Memory Journal for
EVERY GEEKY FIRST
in Your Baby's Life

Tim Mucci

adamsmedia
Avon, Massachusetts

Published by
Adams Media, a division of F+W Media, Inc.
57 Littlefield Street, Avon, MA 02322. U.S.A.
www.adamsmedia.com

ISBN 10: 1-4405-8619-5
ISBN 13: 978-1-4405-8619-4
eISBN 10: 1-4405-8620-9
eISBN 13: 978-1-4405-8620-0

Printed in the United States of America.

10   9   8   7   6   5   4   3   2   1

Library of Congress Cataloging-in-Publication Data

Mucci, Tim.
  The geek baby book / Tim Mucci.
      pages cm
  ISBN 978-1-4405-8619-4 (pob) -- ISBN 1-4405-8619-5 (pob) -- ISBN 978-1-4405-8620-0 (ebook) -- ISBN 1-4405-8620-9 (ebook)
1. Baby books. 2. Infants--Development. I. Title.
HQ779.M83 2015
305.232--dc23
                          2014039909

Cover design by Frank Rivera.
Cover image © iStockphoto.com/Yasna Ten.
Interior Images: Pixel kids and map © Eric Andrews; © iStockphoto.com/ MaryLB, Prikhnenko, pma2010, AdrianHillman, fraserd, YasnaTen, pinnacle-animates, photka, omergenc, sohappywo, sntpzh, miren, sv_sunny, krulUA, ChrisGorgio, MarthaVaculikova; © 123RF/canicula, Boiko Ilia, astrozombie, David Makings, Tomasz Pacyna, Gintaras Svalbonas, multirealism, Tul Chalothonrangsee, Liubou Yasiukovich, Iryna Znoba, Oleksandr Yeromin, anthonycz, yupiramos, jushiung.

This book is available at quantity discounts for bulk purchases.
For information, please call 1-800-289-0963.

Right now, in this galaxy . . .

Fans of comic books, science fiction, fantasy, and horror have found their voices, and they're changing the world. It's never been this easy to be a geek, and being a geek has never been this acceptable.

There are zero books out there that will teach you how to raise a baby who's happy, healthy, *and* a well-adjusted geek. This book isn't even going to try for that first part; there are plenty of manuals for babies out there. You'll probably want to pick up one of those if you haven't done so already. But this one—*this* one is different. (A word of warning, though: The old baby book that's written by Spock is by an entirely different Spock, not the logical, green-blooded Vulcan we know and love.)

What you're holding in your hands right now will help you remember all of those wonderful moments you and your child will share. Hopefully it will also help you to raise a happy, healthy, and well-rounded geek.

Why Grow a Geek?

Because geeks are awesome, that's why.

+ A geek is comfortable with putting in effort to attain enjoyment. A geek very rarely regards entertainment as passive.
+ When geeks love something they immerse themselves in it.
+ Geeks feel strongly about things, and they know what they're talking about.
+ Geeks create costumes and communities. They create empires.

If you grow a geek, you'll get an imaginative child who may be a little more focused, a little more intense, a little more introspective, and, with your help, a little more accepting of others. It's your job as the geek parent to assure your kid that her or his interests are worthwhile, that she's not doing anything wrong, and that some people just will never understand.

Teach your children:

+ That they should use their geek powers for good and never evil
+ That no matter how other people treat them, they should always set the best example
+ That they should be as inclusive as possible
+ That they should never mock someone who knows less than them
+ That the fastest way to build more geeks and a healthy geek culture is to share their passions and hobbies

Some people think geeks never amount to anything, that they're destined to be mere basement dwellers, troglodytes haunting their parent's garages and attics. Not true! Geeks have an amazing pedigree! The list of geeks who have gone on to become famous and powerful cultural figures is long and varied. Here are a few, along with their geek passions:

Name	Job	Geek Thing
Stephen Colbert	Entertainer	Role-playing gamer
Robin Williams	Actor/comedian	Video gamer
Danica McKellar	Actor/author	Math-head
Aisha Tyler	Actor	Video gamer
Nicolas Cage	Actor	Comic book enthusiast
Rosario Dawson	Actor	Comic book enthusiast
H.G. Wells	Author	War gamer
Wil Wheaton	Entertainer	Everything
Vin Diesel	Actor	Role-playing gamer
Rivers Cuomo	Musician	Role-playing gamer

Welcoming Your Little Geek Into the World

That thing that just spent nine months gestating within you or your spouse is out, and it's coming to stay at your house. Don't get too freaked out; I know that it sounds like a monster-of-the-week episode of the *X-Files*, but it's not! No, it's your baby, and it's here to stay.

There are some very important things that you need to do when you first bring your baby home. Yeah, sure, safety things, but you can read another book for that stuff.

What to Name Your Baby

First things first—this kid needs a name. Give it one of those right away. It's important because you're going to want to know what to call it.

Can't think of a name? Well, don't panic. I understand how hard it is to name things; it takes me *hours* to decide what to name my D&D characters. To help you with this important decision, I've provided a handy chart. You can pick and choose at will, or you can roll some dice and see what names come up. Hey, if a random name is good enough for my past few *Dragon Age* characters, it's good enough for your baby.

RANDOM NAME GENERATOR

There are a few methods you can use when rolling on the Random Name Generator charts. First, choose which chart you'd like to roll on, then pick one of the following three methods.

1. Roll two six-sided dice (2d6). It will help if the two dice are different colors, one to indicate rows, and one to indicate columns. Roll the dice, find the intersection of the row number and column number you've rolled, and there's your name.

2. Roll one six-sided die twice, once for row, once for column, and locate the intersection of the row number and column number you've rolled.

3. (Random Awesomeness chart only) For the Random Awesomeness chart, select one of the previous methods and do it twice to get a bad-ass compound name worthy of the most fearsome adventurers. For example, Brienne Moxy-Vision is a pretty great name. Feel free to swap the words around for greater effect.

BOYS' NAMES					
	1	**2**	**3**	**4**	**5**	**6**
1	Dagon	Archer	Tywin	Peter	Walter	Indiana
2	Steve	Zoidberg	Fox	Clark	Kal-El	Max
3	Ambrose	Jor-El	Bruce	The Humongous	Harry	Tron
4	Tanis	Weyland	Edwin	Thor	Howard	Roman
5	Flint	Rex	Han	Red	Sherlock	Luke
6	Kumar	Loki	Xbalanque	Homer	Theon	Mycroft

GIRLS' NAMES						
	1	2	3	4	5	6
1	Lara	Marge	Lana	Dana	Natasha	Arya
2	Delphine	Brienne	Hippolyta	Athena	Xeni	Diana
3	Tasha	Kara	Caitlyn	Mulan	Leia	Irene
4	Joan	Kali	Kaylee	Boudica	Buffy	Belit
5	Zenobia	Ishtar	Devi	Teela	Aurora	Artemis
6	Ellen	Ahsoka	Yuki	Mara	Dorothy	Cordelia

RANDOM AWESOMENESS CHART						
	1	2	3	4	5	6
1	Lightning	Heart	No	Doctor	Seven	Claw
2	Power	Maul	Wolf	Winter	Stomper	Moxy
3	Doom	Who	Bolt	Vision	Wild	Hammer
4	Blade	Blue	Snow	Argent	Saint	Flame
5	Explosion	War	Peace	Shout	Beast	Nothing
6	Enigma	Shade	Grin	Shatter	Skull	Stone

Decorating the Baby's Room

You should also think about decorating your baby's room. You want to make sure your little geekling is swaddled tight within his very own Fortress of Solitude, right?

To start, you can create a spinning mobile out of your old Teenage Mutant Ninja Turtles action figures. If the thought of unpackaging and stringing up your mint-condition collectibles appalls you, remember that you're a parent now, and you should start passing down the things you love to your children so that they can experience that same unbridled awe that you experienced when encountering them, Kung-Fu grip and all. Now is your chance to nurture your baby with all of those things that comfort you.

Put some comic art up on the walls. Frame that animation cell from *Batman: The Animated Series*, and find a place to hang it. Plug in the TARDIS nightlight, and make sure baby hugs that plush Minecraft Creeper all night long. He's sure to sleep like a . . . well . . . baby.

Now that you have a name for your kid, let's sit back and take stock of things.

YOU ARE NOW IN CHARGE OF A O-LEVEL HUMAN

Please fill out the character record sheet to determine your 0-level human's basic characteristics.

NAME: -

SEX: -

RACE (HUMAN): -

LEVEL: -

EXPERIENCE POINTS: -

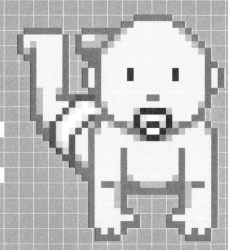

Character Sheet

Movement: 10' (crawl) _____

Time born: _____

Place of origin: _____

Hospital: _____

Patron Deity: _____

Alignment (check one)

☐ Lawful ☐ Chaotic ☐ Neutral

Class
(check one)

☐ Fighter   Hair: _____
☐ Wizard   Eyes: _____
☐ Baby
☐ Thief
☐ Cleric

Character Portrait or Symbol

Attributes
(Roll 2d6 to determine)

CUTENESS: _____

GIGGLE: _____

STINKINESS: _____

STRENGTH: _____

DEXTERITY: _____

WISDOM: _____

Armor Class
(DEX + CUTE)

Hit Points
(DEX + STR)

Saving Throws

✦ Death Ray/Magic Wand: 20%
✦ Spit up: 10%
✦ Dragon Breath: 40%
✦ Eat Hands/Feet: 5%
✦ Grab Finger: 50%

Proficiencies

(You have 10 points to allocate toward proficiencies. For a 0-level human baby, no single proficiency can exceed 3.)

Burping: _____

Notice hands/feet: _____

Sleeping: _____

Not sleeping: _____

Smiling: _____

Rolling over: _____

Languages

(Check any your 0-level human would know.)

☐ Baby
☐ Common
☐ Goblin
☐ Klingon

Spells

☐ Aura of Cuteness
☐ Piercing Shriek
☐ Stinking Cloud

Equipment:

_____

_____

_____

Money and Treasure (Gifts and Presents):

_____

_____

_____

_____

_____

Background

You have now completed your 0-level human's character sheet. As a human, your child starts with no penalties or bonuses. She's not limited as to what character class she can become, nor does she have any minimum or maximum to any of her attributes. Gender does not affect her statistics or attributes.

To get a better idea about who your human is, it might be helpful to answer some of the following questions.

OMINOUS PORTENTS DURING/AFTER BIRTH:

- ☐ Attacked by evil wizard
- ☐ Blood moon
- ☐ Animals speaking prophecies
- ☐ Faerie pact
- ☐ Visit from future self
- ☐ None
- ☐ Other: ....

WHICH OF THESE SKILLS HAS THE BABY MASTERED?

- ☐ Recognizing parent's voice
- ☐ Smiling
- ☐ Laughing
- ☐ Baby grip
- ☐ Cooing
- ☐ Kung fu
- ☐ Invisibility

HOW DID THE BABY COME INTO THE WORLD?

- ☐ Successful birthing ritual
- ☐ Hatched from alien chrysalis
- ☐ Parthenogenesis
- ☐ Sprang from the head of a Titan
- ☐ That thing that the Doctor does
- ☐ Respawned at spawn point
- ☐ From the ashes of an earlier iteration
- ☐ Other: ....

*Read on to see what class
your human might be.*

BY WHAT MANNER OF CONVEYANCE DID BABY COME HOME?

- ☐ Vigilante car
- ☐ Back of a dragon
- ☐ Magic spell
- ☐ Flight:
  - ☐ Wings
  - ☐ Telekinesis
  - ☐ Teleportation
  - ☐ Device
  - ☐ Spell
- ☐ Time Machine
- ☐ Police Box
- ☐ Sports Car
- ☐ Phone Booth
- ☐ Pocket Watch
- ☐ Other: ....

WHERE DOES BABY SLEEP?

- ☐ Bio-organic cocoon
- ☐ Doesn't; just sits and stares quietly all night
- ☐ Hanging upside down from the rafters
- ☐ Crib
- ☐ Other: ....

CLASSES

Your 0-level human may be eligible for some starting-class specializations.

Answer these questions to see where he may fit.

Jedi Knight

Midi-chlorian count: ....
(Ask your doctor to provide. 2,500 = normal human)

SPONTANEOUSLY LEVITATES OBJECTS?
☐ Yes
☐ No

ASTHMATIC CYBORG?
☐ Yes
☐ No

PROPHESIED TO BRING BALANCE TO THE FORCE?
☐ Yes
☐ No

Wizard

INVITATION TO HOGWARTS?
☐ Yes
☐ No

PARSELMOUTH?
☐ Yes
☐ No

DISTINCTLY SHAPED SCAR?
☐ Crescent
☐ Star
☐ Ominous string of numbers
☐ Lightning bolt
☐ Angelic sigil
☐ None
☐ Other: ....

SUPERHUMAN

SPONTANEOUSLY LEVITATES OBJECTS?
☐ Yes
☐ No

LIFTS COUCHES, CRIB, REFRIGERATORS, TRUCKS, OTHER ABOVE HEAD?
☐ Yes
☐ No

BEAMS SHOOT FROM EYES?
☐ Heat
☐ Cold
☐ None
☐ Other: ....

CAN FLY?
☐ Yes
☐ No

HAS SUPER SPEED?
☐ Yes
☐ No

OTHER HINTS OF POWERS AND ABILITIES:

....

....

....

TIME LORD

ODDLY DISTINCTIVE WARDROBE?
☐ Yes
☐ No

If yes, describe:

....

....

NATURE?
☐ Mischievous
☐ Serious
☐ Whimsical
☐ Other: ....

SONIC SCREWDRIVER?
☐ Yes
☐ No

TIME AND RELATIVE DIMENSIONS IN SPACE MACHINE?
☐ Yes
☐ No

POLICE PUBLIC CALL BOX

Slayer (GIRLS ONLY)

STRONGER THAN NORMAL?
- ☐ Yes
- ☐ No

CAN SENSE VAMPIRES/DANGER?
- ☐ Yes
- ☐ No

HAS A WATCHER?
- ☐ Yes
- ☐ No

Various Skills and Abilities:

DID BABY SPEAK JUST AFTER BEING BORN?
- ☐ Yes
- ☐ No

IF YES, WHAT DID BABY SAY?
- ☐ By Grabthar's hammer!
- ☐ Ph'nglui mglw'nafh Cthulhu R'lyeh wgah'nagl fhtagn
- ☐ Shazam!
- ☐ Other: ....

WORDS OF WISDOM

"The best way to guide children without

coercion is to be ourselves."

—MADELEINE L'ENGLE, *A CIRCLE OF QUIET*

Your baby has been born! It's time to document this awesome event. Don't you want to remember the time you created a human without having to harness the power of lightning, make arcane pacts, or build one out of clay in the hope that some deific force would imbue it with life? If having a baby is anything like having a cat, you'll be taking lots of pictures to post on the Internet, and you'll likely have one or two that you'll want to keep. Maybe the scientists at the lab, the doctors at the hospital, or the Jedi elder who attended the birth took a photo or recorded the event on a holocron. Tape them in the following pages:

PHOTOGRAPHIC EVIDENCE

WORDS OF WISDOM

"Children have never been very good at listening to their elders, but they have never failed to imitate them."

—JAMES BALDWIN

IT IS THE YEAR ....

It is the year _____, the year your geekling has joined the vast collective of humanity on the planet Earth. Interesting things are happening all the time, and the year of your geekling's birth is no exception to that rule. If it is . . . well, as Sherlock Holmes once said, "An exception disproves the rule." Fill out the stuff here, so your little rule breaker can always remember it.

GOVERNMENT LEADERS:

....

....

....

....

PLANETARY OVERLORDS:

....

....

....

....

TRUE NAMES OF THE MEMBERS OF THE SECRET SOCIETY THAT REALLY RULE THE WORLD:

....

....

....

....

MAJOR NEWS EVENTS:

....

....

....

....

....

....

MINOR NEWS EVENTS:

....

....

RANDOM HAPPENINGS AROUND THE HOUSE:

....

....

THINGS PEOPLE LOVE THIS YEAR:

....

....

....

THINGS PEOPLE HATE THIS YEAR:

....

....

....

BEST MOVIE OF THE YEAR:

....

BEST BOOK OF THE YEAR:

....

BEST COMIC/GRAPHIC NOVEL OF THE YEAR:

....

BEST TV SERIES THIS YEAR:

....

OTHER NOTEWORTHY EVENTS:

....

....

....

....

VISITORS

People love to look at babies. They love to poke them, hold them, talk to them, put them in their mouths, pretend to steal them, and gift them with amazing powers or incredible destinies. There has yet to be a baby born who hasn't drawn the gaze of a crowd of cooing, squealing onlookers. It doesn't matter if your geekling was found in a crashed rocket ship or was carried home lovingly from the hospital, people will want to look at her. Here's a nifty spot to list all of those first visitors:

FAMILY AND FRIENDS:

....

....

....

....

....

....

EXTRATERRESTRIALS:

....

....

GODS/DEMIGODS:

....

VARIOUS OTHER NON-HUMAN ENTITIES:

....

GIFTS RECEIVED:

....

....

....

....

PROPHECIES MADE:

....

....

There and Back Again: Mementos and Memories

Your geekling is brand new to the world, so every day for him is going to be an adventure. He's experiencing everything for the very first time, and each outing is an epic undertaking that's every bit as exciting as the greatest superhero origin story. He'll be learning new things, absorbing the world around him and acquiring helpful skills that will aid him in future adventures.

Since every day is a new adventure, why not keep a record of the strange lands traveled by your geekling? Use the map and chart your little adventurer's journeys, missteps, milestones, great battles, and fantastic treasures.

Every adventurer needs a chronicler of their heroic deeds and exploits. That chronicler is you! Be sure to take lots of notes and mark the map carefully so your geekling will know where he's been, and the amazing works he's accomplished.

"YOUR MOTHER'S DEAD.
BEFORE LONG I'LL BE DEAD,
AND YOU AND YOUR BROTHER
AND YOUR SISTER AND ALL OF HER
CHILDREN, ALL OF US DEAD,
ALL OF US ROTTING UNDERGROUND.
IT'S THE FAMILY NAME THAT LIVES ON.
IT'S ALL THAT LIVES ON.
NOT YOUR PERSONAL GLORY,
NOT YOUR HONOR . . . BUT FAMILY."

—Tywin Lannister on family, from *Game of Thrones*: Season One, Episode Seven, "You Win or You Die"

First Crawl _____

First Steps _____

First Word _____

First Smile _____

First Rolled Over _____

First Doctor's Appointment _____

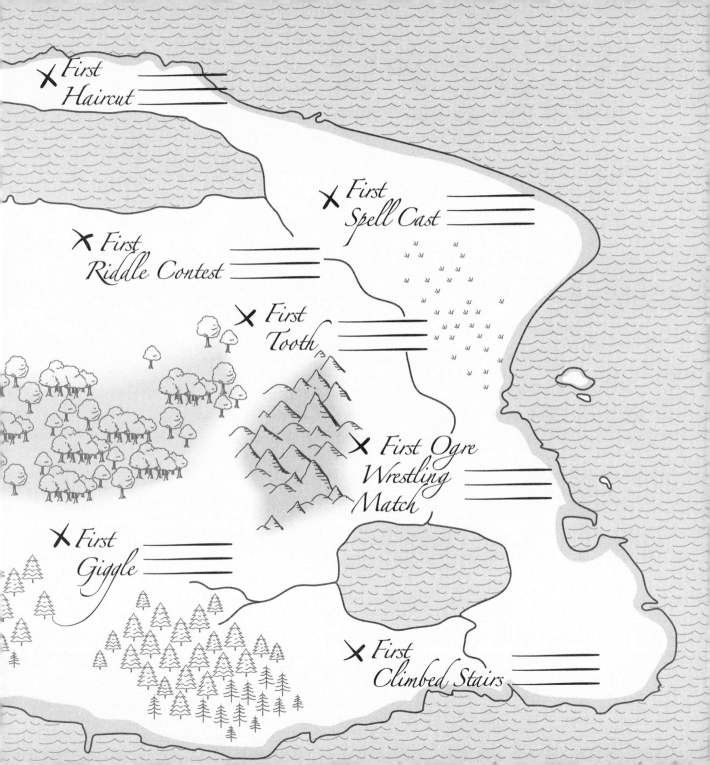

X *First Haircut* _____

X *First Spell Cast* _____

X *First Riddle Contest* _____

X *First Tooth* _____

X *First Ogre Wrestling Match* _____

X *First Giggle* _____

X *First Climbed Stairs* _____

RELIGIOUS CEREMONIES

Almost every family has some sort of ritual or tradition to welcome their baby into the world; why should a geek family be any different? As geeks we're steeped in matters historical, mythological, and imaginative, and what is religion if not an amalgamation of all of those things? Some of us adhere to one of the world's major religions, while others proclaim ourselves adepts of the Force, Robotology, or scientific theory itself. The point is, we've all got belief systems. Because, after all, our geekling may very well be the next Messiah, Kwisatz Haderach, Nobel Prize winner, or one who will bring balance to the Force. Why take the chance? List your observances and important dates here.

GEEK RESPONSIBILITY

RESPONSIBILITIES OF A GEEK PARENT

There are certain responsibilities that come with being a geek parent. Sure, changing diapers and stuff, but if you want to learn that, go watch a YouTube video. No, you're the parent of a geek, and you have a higher calling. You are molding the next generation of geeks in an environment that's tailor made for them. From their very first steps, they'll wield the power of the Internet. Before long, they'll be connecting to the world in amazing ways. They'll develop passions for things that will seem almost alien to you, but you'll also be passing down your own geek loves and passions. All of this sharing should be recorded. Do that here.

FIRST SONG YOU SHARED: ....

FIRST GAME YOU PLAYED TOGETHER: ....

FIRST FANTASY FILM OR CARTOON YOU WATCHED TOGETHER: ....

FIRST THING YOU LAUGHED AT TOGETHER: ....

FAVORITE MOVIE TO WATCH TOGETHER: ....

FAVORITE BOOK TO READ TOGETHER: ....

THINGS YOU LEARNED FROM ONE ANOTHER: ....

....

....

....

GEEK LOVE

Everyone knows that geeks love to share their interests with other geeks, family members, and random people on the street. We wear it on our T-shirts and hats, and it's even in the slang we use. As the parent of a geek, and an obviously intelligent person (you bought this book, didn't you?), you're probably into some pretty cool things yourself. Let's delve into what makes the parents of a geek so cool.

NAMES: .... + ...

HOW DID YOU MEET?
- ☐ During a raid in World of Warcraft
- ☐ At San Diego Comic-Con
- ☐ At New York Comic Con
- ☐ Other con: ....

HOW DID YOU KNOW THAT THIS GEEK WAS FOR YOU?
- ☐ Both were wearing the same cosplay
- ☐ Both were wearing the same EFF T-shirt
- ☐ Both posted the same comment on a message board/YouTube video
- ☐ Members of the same club or Meetup group
- ☐ Other: ....

WHICH TV SERIES DID YOU FIRST BOND OVER?
- ☐ *X-Files*
- ☐ *Firefly*
- ☐ *Buffy the Vampire Slayer*
- ☐ *Star Trek*
- ☐ *Game of Thrones*
- ☐ *Supernatural*
- ☐ *Doctor Who*
- ☐ Other: ....

WHEN DID YOU BECOME GEEK-MATES?
....

HOW DID YOU OFFICIALLY PAIR UP?
- ☐ Religious ceremony
- ☐ Pon farr
- ☐ Archenemies who fell in love
- ☐ Other: ....

WORDS OF WISDOM

"There is no point in being grown up if you can't be childish sometimes."

—THE DOCTOR, *DR. WHO*

THE FANTASTIC FAMILY

Your geek family should be like your very own super team. The Avengers has a leader in Steve Rogers/Captain America, a brilliant scientist in Bruce Banner/The Hulk, a genius inventor in Tony Stark/Iron Man, and courageous fighters in Natasha Romanov/Black Widow and Clint Barton/Hawkeye. Each member of your family will have different powers and abilities, and your geekling will round out the team, learning quickly from both you and her own experiences out in the world. With each day that passes, she'll become more powerful, more unique, and a more integral part of your little super team. Here's a place to list some of those newfound powers and the date they manifested.

BABY'S SPECIAL ABILITIES:

POWER TO SIT UP:　　/　　/

POWER TO CRAWL:　　/　　/

　HOW:
　☐ Normal
　☐ Up walls
　☐ Faster than a speeding bullet
　☐ Through time

POWER TO WALK:　　/　　/

POWER TO SPEAK:　　/　　/

FIRST WORD: ....

　LANGUAGE WORD WAS SPOKEN IN:
　☐ Klingon　　☐ Aklo
　☐ Elvish　　☐ Simlish
　☐ Esperanto　☐ Other:
　☐ Parseltongue　.........................

CATCHPHRASES:
☐ Resistance is futile.
☐ Bazinga!
☐ I have a bad feeling about this.
☐ Frak!
☐ Make it so.
☐ Other: ....

....

POWER TO DRESS SELF:　　/　　/

CHILD DRESSED SELF AS:
☐ Superhero
☐ Steve the Player
☐ The Doctor
☐ Jedi
☐ Hobbit
☐ Other: ....

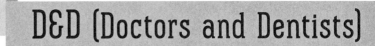

Keeping track of your geekling's health information is very important. A happy and successful geek is a healthy geek. Unless your geekling has Wolverine's healing ability or absorbs the yellow radiation of Earth's sun to become invulnerable, she's going to need to see the doctor and dentist regularly. Record all of baby's health information here.

IMMUNIZATIONS AND BOOSTER SHOTS RECEIVED AGAINST:

☐ Zombie plague
☐ Andromeda Strain
☐ Captain Trips
☐ Dragon Pox
☐ Greyscale
☐ Legacy Virus (affects mutants only)
☐ Spattergroit
☐ St. Mary's virus
☐ Others:.....................................

ILLNESSES AND ACCIDENTS:

☐ Bombarded by gamma rays
☐ Bitten by radioactive insect
☐ Hit by lighting/doused by chemical/gained super-speed
☐ Others: ....

DENTAL RECORD:

FIRST BABY TOOTH: / /

FIRST FANGS: / /

FIRST BABY TOOTH LOST: / /

FIRST VISIT TO DENTIST: / /

TEETH MADE OF:

☐ Metal
☐ Ceramic
☐ Enamel
☐ Lasers

FOOD

It's popularly supposed that we geeks don't always have the best of diets. After all, we spend so much time dedicating our-selves to being the best it is at what we do—which is sometimes not pretty—that occasionally we end up eating fast, not-so-nutritious food. If your baby is going to grow up to be a strong, healthy, empire-building geek, it's best to make sure he's eating right. Start by shelving the Mountain Dew and Red Vines for the next eighteen years or so. Record your healthy baby food choices here.

SOME FOOD LIKES:

SOME FOOD DISLIKES:

FIRST TIME USING UTENSILS: / /

FIRST TIME DRINKING FROM A CUP: / /

FIRST SOLID FOOD: / /
- ☐ Lembas bread
- ☐ Soylent Green
- ☐ Spam
- ☐ More Spam
- ☐ Other:

WORDS OF WISDOM

"The best way to make children good is

to make them happy."

—OSCAR WILDE

An Open Letter to the Parents of a Geek-to-Be

Your Star Wars responsibility . . .

A clear staple of geek culture is the near-universal adoration for the original three Star Wars films. They are the standard to which many current science fiction, adventure, and fantasy films are held. They embody mythic storytelling; they evoke a simpler time and recast the strong-jawed heroes and buxom waifs of the space operas that came before; and they depict scrappy farm kids, morally gray scoundrels, and courageous royalty. It is, as the *Epic of Gilgamesh* was to the Mesopotamians, an epic in our lifetime.

Episodes IV, V, and VI are classic films and should be enjoyed with the entire family. Your responsibility as a parent, keeping the legacy of the Star Wars universe untainted, is this:

Never let your children watch Episodes I, II, and III.

It's a controversial opinion, I know, but you'll have to trust me—a life without Jar Jar Binks is a good life indeed.

Of course, your kid will eventually find out that the prequel episodes exist, perhaps from being astute enough to notice that *A New Hope* starts with the words "Episode IV," or just by simply living in an age of constantly fluid information.

If they ask about Episodes I–III, sit them down and show them the movie *The Ring*—or something else that will terrify them and stop them asking questions about the first three episodes of Star Wars. If they persist, tell them that they must have slipped into an alternate reality where those movies were never made.

If they can see through this ruse, then you must take the ultimate step in parental responsibility and *never let them see those movies*!

Instead, use this as an opportunity to bond geek-to-geek. Engage their imagination and your own by viewing the movies alone beforehand, finding the good parts, teasing out the intrigue and the characters, and then telling it to your young geek Jedi apprentice as a story. Take the movies that we have, and make them into what they should have been. Share with your kids that sense of wonder you felt about Star Wars as a kid.

Tell them the story of how the power-hungry Darth Sidious masqueraded as the kindly Senator Palpatine and clawed his way up from senator to emperor, leaving the galaxy shattered and subjugated. Tell them the story of Anakin Skywalker, a troubled young warrior, gifted with power, used and manipulated by both friend and foe. Tell them the tale of Obi-Wan Kenobi, a brash and capable young man thrust into responsibility he wasn't ready for, and wasn't strong enough to master. Or of Padmé Amidala, a courageous ruler, unafraid to wield political and martial power, who is undone by love.

Embellish and retcon, fix plot holes, and flesh out characters. Make it epic and stirring, and eventually when your kids finally do see Episodes I, II, and III, they'll always think, "My parents' version was better."

Of course, the reality is that as a geek, you'll be happy watching Episodes I–III with your geeklings. For all their flaws, they're fun to watch as a family. And of course, when you finally relent, you can also share the excellent *Star Wars: The Clone Wars* animated series with them, for which it's totally worth sitting through the prequel movies.

WORDS OF WISDOM

"When a man dies, if he can pass

enthusiasm along to his children, he has

left them an estate of incalculable value."

—THOMAS EDISON

Family Tree

As geeks, we have a built-in tribe that is determined by the things we're geeky about. Browncoats gather under the banner of the Firefly-class ship captained by Mal Reynolds. Whovians bounce around space and time in a blue police box with the immortal and mercurial Doctor. The Slayers of prophecy have Watchers and Scooby gangs looking out for them . . . and the list goes on. Whether you're a Trekkie or a gamer, we all come from somewhere and we all belong someplace. Slytherin House, perhaps, or beneath the direwolf banner of House Stark of Winterfell. Here is where you may record your geekling's grand family history, family words, and amazing exploits of geeks past and present.

1. Write name of your geekling in the banner above the large blank shield at the top of the following page.

2. Draw the coat of arms of your house inside of the large blank shield at the top of the page.

3. Write your house words or motto in the lines at the bottom of the large blank shield.

4. Above each of the smaller shields, write the name of a relative and how that person is related to your geekling.

5. Within each of the smaller blank shields, feel free to draw a coat of arms and write house words for each person, especially if his or her "house" is different from yours.

6. Underneath the name of each person, write one or two geeky things about him or her.

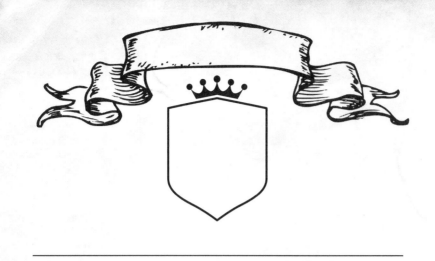

_____

house _____

house _____

_____

house _____ house _____ house _____ house _____

_____

house _____

_____

_____

house _____

_____

_____

house _____

_____

_____

house _____

_____

_____

house _____

_____

_____

house _____

_____

_____

house _____

_____

_____

house _____

_____

_____

house _____

_____

_____

house _____

_____

_____

house _____

_____

_____

house _____

_____

_____

LEVEL UP!

It's time to see how much your geekling has grown. You've had some adventures together by now, faced monsters, and gotten to know your family line. It's time to calculate your experience points and see if your geekling has hit Level One.

HEIGHT: _____ **HAIR:** _____

GEEKIEST MOMENT SO FAR: _____

_____

COLLECTIBLES BOUGHT: _____

_____

LAWS OF THE UNIVERSE BROKEN: _____

_____

FAVORITE WORDS TO SAY: _____

_____

FAVORITE GEEK THINGS TO DO: _____

_____

FIRST BIRTHDAY

It's a birthday! It's time to celebrate an entire year of your geekling's hard work being born and learning how the world works. Bake a cake, wrap some presents, invite some friends, blow up some balloons, drink some juice, and get ready to party hard.

WHAT KIND OF CELEBRATION DID YOU HAVE FOR BABY'S FIRST BIRTHDAY?

☐ Party
☐ Dinner
☐ Cotillion
☐ Pod race
☐ Wild boar hunt
☐ Other ....

PRESENTS RECEIVED:

WHO ATTENDED:

GAMES PLAYED:

BEST PART OF THE BIRTHDAY:

WORST PART OF THE BIRTHDAY:

HAIR

Hairstyles are very prominent in geek culture. The fourth Doctor had wonderful curly hair. Natasha Romanov, the Black Widow from the Avengers, styles her flaming red hair in many different ways. Wolverine from the X-Men keeps his hair in a wild, wing-like style. How will your geekling style her hair? Here are a few fun ways to choose from.

The Marge Simpson

The Thor

Mullet
(business up front, party in the rear)

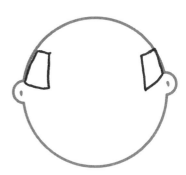

The Wolverine

The Mr. T

The Picard

My geekling's hair

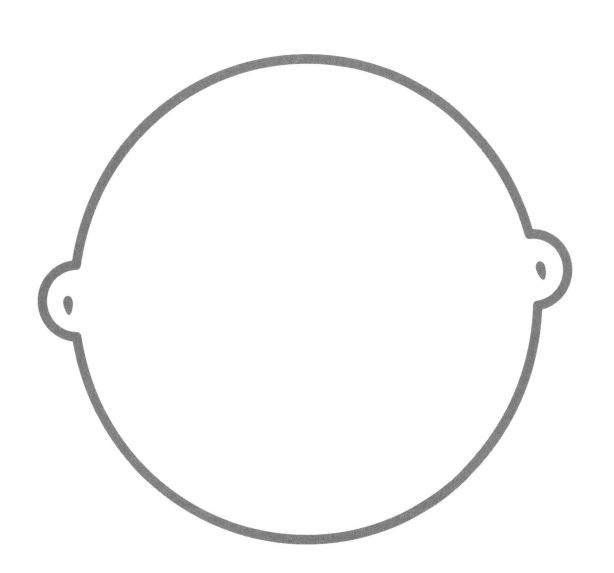

My geekling's first haircut

FIRST HAIRCUT: /   /

HOW DID BABY RESPOND:

....

....

....

PHOTOGRAPHIC EVIDENCE:

HERE BE MONSTERS

This is a tricky one. Children aren't supposed to like monsters. They're supposed to be afraid of them, right? You're not the parent of a mere child though. Your young padawan is a geek! A young geek has the propensity to never be afraid of monsters, because monsters are interesting things. They have fur and claws and horns. They have sharp teeth, sometimes multiple eyes. Sometimes they're small, sometimes they're huge. Sometimes they have weird powers or wield strange technology. Sometimes they're good, and sometimes they're really bad, but monsters are always interesting.

FIRST MONSTER: ....

FAVORITE MONSTER: ....

FAVORITE THING ABOUT MONSTER: ....

....

....

FIRST SCARY MONSTER: ....

WHY WAS IT SCARY? ....

....

....

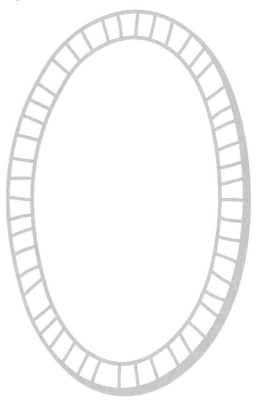

Draw a cool monster in the space provided.

FIRST TOYS AND GAMES

A geek's life is one that will most likely be filled with toys and gadgets. Play will never be frowned upon, because a geek knows that playing with toys, games, words, paint, or film means using creativity to understand the world around him. Your geekling will learn this, and he'll also learn that play is okay no matter how young or how old you are. He'll learn this, because you're going to teach him!

Start out simple. You won't get great results if the first thing you do with your geekling is break out your *B2: The Keep on the Borderlands* D&D module. Start with nesting dolls and colored blocks—make sure some of those early shapes are polyhedral, and get your geekling used to rolling them—then move on to puzzles, board games, and eventually strategy games.

Your geekling's first toys will be the tools with which he'll start to parse the world.

GEEKLING'S FAVORITE TOY:

....

SECOND FAVORITE TOY:

....

FAVORITE WAY TO PLAY WITH THE TOY:
- ☐ Like a baby
- ☐ Take it apart and put it back together again
- ☐ Use it to create a device that bends the laws of physics
- ☐ Other:

....

LEAST FAVORITE TOY:

....

MOST EXPENSIVE TOY THAT BABY WON'T PLAY WITH:

....

FIRST GAME PLAYED:

....

FIRST GAME WON: ....

FIRST GAME LOST: ....

FIRST TIME BEING A SORE LOSER: /   /

FIRST TIME BEING A SORE WINNER: /   /

FIRST GAME CHEATED AT: ....

FIRST TIME ROLLING A NATURAL 20:   /   /

FIRST COLLECTIBLE TOY: ....
- ✦ How much toy is worth in one year: ....
- ✦ How much toy is worth in five years: ....
- ✦ Date toy was sold for rent money: /   /

WORDS OF WISDOM

"Being a mother is an attitude,

not a biological relation."

—ROBERT A. HEINLEIN,
HAVE SPACE SUIT, WILL TRAVEL

FIRST QUEST

Your geekling is fortunate in that the world of quests is new to her. She can look forward to a long life of questing for something. Maybe a science degree. Maybe the first issue of a rare comic, to master a musical instrument, or to find a magic ring that turns the wearer invisible. All adventurers have a first adventure, and you'll get to be there as your geekling goes on hers. You get to be her Nick Fury, Gandalf, or Morpheus. The truth is, if you're doing it right, dangerous adventures will be hard to come by for a baby. But it's still worth chronicling your child's first few exploits, mundane as they may be. Write them down here, and don't be afraid to liberally apply adjectives.

FIRST TIME OUTSIDE IN THE WORLD:

HOW DID GEEKLING REACT?

WHAT WAS GEEKLING'S FAVORITE PART?

WAS ANYTHING SCARY?

WAS ANYTHING AMAZING?

HOW MANY NINJAS WERE DEFEATED?

comics

The world of comics is an eminently geeky one filled with all manner of characters and genres. It's one that is becoming more and more popular with each blockbuster movie based on a comic book superhero, like Batman, the Avengers, or the X-Men. Even non-superhero comic books have found critical acclaim, both in their original form and as movies: *Ghost World, A History of Violence*, Neil Gaiman's Sandman series, or *Road to Perdition*. Comic geeks know these vast worlds by heart, are able to talk in depth about storylines that span decades, and know which comic company (DC, Marvel, or one of the many independent houses) publishes these comics. Not all geeks are comic geeks, but your geekling shouldn't be left in the dark about comics just because you've never enlightened yourself on the subject.

See how much you know about comics by taking the quiz, then add up the score and see how fit you are to be the parent of a comic geek.

1. This DC superhero has no super powers, has an endless supply of money, and loves to dress up like a monster and hit people.

Match the hero with his or her description. Each correct answer is worth 10 points.

SPIDER-MAN

SUPERMAN

BATMAN

WONDER WOMAN

THE TICK

CAPTAIN MARVEL

WOLVERINE

CEREBUS

BLACK WIDOW

THE FLASH

5. This Marvel hero is a high school nerd who, after accidentally being injured during a science experiment, gained great strength and the ability to stick to walls.

----

2. This DC hero is an alien who landed on Earth as a baby, was raised by humans, then became a reporter. The earth's yellow sun makes him very strong and hard to hurt, but he's allergic to green rocks.

----

4. This DC hero can run and move really, really fast. His last name isn't Gordon, but he does wear red and yellow.

----

6. This Marvel hero was a member of the United States Air Force until her genes were fused with alien Kree DNA. She gained powers including flight and super strength, and has had multiple heroic identities.

----

3. This DC hero was born on an island of women warriors, was given powers by the gods, and was sent to our world as an emissary of peace. Her main weapons are a lasso and indestructible bracelets.

----

7. This Marvel hero is a globetrotting secret agent, an ex-KGB assassin who now fights alongside earth's mightiest heroes, the Avengers. Her trademark look includes red hair and a black bodysuit.

----

8. This Marvel hero has a healing factor that's been keeping him alive for centuries. He was kidnapped by a mysterious government agency known as Department K, who laced his bones with indestructible metal in an attempt to turn him into the perfect weapon.

----

9. This aardvark of independent comics starred in a 300-issue-long series, which tackled everything from genre parodies to politics and religion.

----

10. This hero wears the mantle of a giant blue bug and is quite possibly insane. He is the protector of The City, and hangs around with an accountant who dresses like a moth.

SCORE: ------------------

100—CONGRATULATIONS! Your kid will be so comic savvy that she'll probably be explaining to all of her friends the intricacies of the entire series run of *Akira*, or *Jimmy Corrigan the Smartest Kid on Earth*. Be proud!

90—GREAT JOB. Your kid will know the various comic book multiverses forward and backward by the time other kids are still plodding through Doctor Seuss.

80—FANTASTIC. This kid will understand exactly what you're talking about when you're ranting about how Captain Marvel should have stayed Captain Marvel because Captain Marvel came first, but Captain Marvel is still a really cool character despite not being the first Captain Marvel.

70—COOL. Your kid is going to be well familiar with the X-Men in all of their various timelines and alternate dimensions.

60—HEY, GREAT. Your kid will at least know the difference between the Flash and Flash Gordon.

50—PRETTY GOOD. You can probably name at least three members of the Legion of Super-Heroes.

40—OKAY, C'MON. Would it kill you to read something published before the year 2008? Comics didn't start with the first Iron Man movie.

30—YEAH, FINE, comics aren't really your thing. Hopefully you have an aunt or brother that can fill in the gaps.

20—I MEAN . . . you probably know Marmaduke, at least?

10—Y'SEE, comics are this thing where there are words and pictures and . . . nevermind.

0—If I could take that kid away from you and get you a subscription to *The Fantastic Four*, I would.

ENTERTAINMENT

One of the many forms of entertainment that you and your geekling will bond over will be movies. There are many science fiction, fantasy, and adventure films that are perfect to share with your little geek. You probably already have your favorites you're just waiting to share, but here are some more classics that are ideal to add to your collection.

FANTASY

+ *The Neverending Story*
+ Chronicles of Narnia
+ *Labyrinth*
+ *Howl's Moving Castle*
+ Harry Potter
+ *The Wizard of Oz*
+ *The Dark Crystal*

SCIENCE FICTION

+ *E.T.*
+ *Back to the Future*
+ *WALL-E*
+ *Lilo & Stitch*
+ *Ghostbusters*
+ *Godzilla vs. Megalon*
+ *The Iron Giant*

ADVENTURE

+ *The Goonies*
+ *The Lego Movie*
+ *Honey, I Shrunk the Kids*
+ *Toy Story* (and *Toy Story 2* and *Toy Story 3*)
+ *Who Framed Roger Rabbit?*
+ *Princess Mononoke*

When your geekling is old enough to travel you'll probably be itching to get out of the Fortress and show him the wide world. Where will your first vacation be? The witch-haunted streets of Arkham, Massachusetts, perhaps? Maybe you'll hop on the back of a great eagle and wing your way to Mount Doom to see baleful Mordor from a safe distance. You could book a ticket to a moon colony, take a road trip to the Grand Canyon, or visit New York to see the skies cluttered with costumed superheroes flying from Avengers headquarters to the next galactic dust-up. Wherever you choose to go, you'll want to make sure you record your thoughts and memories for prosperity. And for time-traveling archaeologists.

ON OUR FIRST VACATION WE WENT:

WHY WE WANTED TO GO:

COOL THINGS WE SAW:

COOLEST PEOPLE WE TALKED TO:

TRAVELED BY:
- ☐ Airplane
- ☐ Car
- ☐ Jetpack
- ☐ Super-speed

BEST PART OF VACATION:

WORST PART OF VACATION:

INTERESTING THINGS WE TOOK BACK WITH US:

NUMBER OF MONSTERS SLAIN:

SUPERHEROES

From the very beginning, people have told stories about humans, gods, and demi-gods questing and fighting against the forces of evil. Modern super-heroic myths like Batman and the Avengers are no different. Superhero movies are now the biggest blockbusters in the theaters, and costumed adventurers grace big screen and small screen alike.

Most geeklings will view their parents as their first heroes, but it's likely they'll also gravitate toward those powered-up women and men who don bright spandex uniforms and give themselves colorful new identities with which to have fantastic adventures. With such great role models, a baby geek is sure to grow up to be a hero.

Draw your geekling's costume on the next page; include symbols, gadgets, and a superhero name.

Having trouble coming up with a superhero name? Use the chart to the right.

POWERS:

CRIME STOPPED:

ARCHENEMY:

FAVORITE SUPERHERO COMIC:

FAVORITE SUPERHERO MOVIE:

FAVORITE SUPERHERO TELEVISION SHOW:

FAVORITE SUPERHERO:

Superhero Name Generator

First letter of baby's first name		First letter of baby's middle or last name	
A	Pink	A	Spider
B	Red	B	Defender
C	Blue	C	Avenger
D	Green	D	Hawk
E	Purple	E	Lantern
F	Fuchsia	F	Thunder
G	Magenta	G	Haze
H	Violet	H	Blade
I	Yellow	I	Sentinel
J	Orange	J	Knight
K	Maroon	K	Wasp
L	Brown	L	Speed
M	Black	M	Ring
N	White	N	Fist
O	Emerald	O	Rock
P	Gray	P	Queen
Q	Crimson	Q	Princess
R	Lilac	R	Eagle
S	Burgundy	S	Talon
T	Hazel	T	Cry
U	Iron	U	Wizard
V	Bronze	V	Wolf
W	Gold	W	Cat
X	Silver	X	Dog
Y	Argent	Y	Scorpion
Z	Sterling	Z	Death

MY GEEKLING'S SUPERHERO COSTUME

BABY'S SUPERHERO NAME:

BOOKS FOR THE BABY

A major part of geek life centers around reading: fantasy novels, Twitter feeds, graphic novels, science texts, and the *Dungeon Master's Guide*. If your geek baby wasn't already reading straight from the womb, they're going to start eventually. Long before they can read, you'll be reading to them. Take this opportunity to entertain them with the books and stories you've always loved. What a great way to relive all of your favorite tales. Here's a list of some books that would be perfect to read to your little captive audience.

Where the Wild Things Are by Maurice Sendak
There's a Nightmare in My Closet by Mercer Mayer
The Cat in the Hat by Dr. Seuss
Vader's Little Princess by Jeffery Brown
The Hobbit by J.R.R. Tolkien
The Giver by Lois Lowry
Matilda by Roald Dahl
The Lion, the Witch, and the Wardrobe by C.S. Lewis
The Hero and the Crown by Robin McKinley
Coraline by Neil Gaiman
The Mighty Miss Malone by Christopher Paul Curtis

There are probably books that you love that aren't listed here. List those here:

....

....

....

....

GEEK RESPONSIBILITY
PARENTS' MANTRA

I'm sure babying will be mostly a piece of cake to a problem-solving machine such as you, but sometimes you'll not be able to quell the Krayt dragon-like squalls of your geekling. You'll have changed so many diapers that your plumbob will be dipping down from green to white and into the red. In times like these, recite the following words, taken directly from *Dune* by Frank Herbert. They helped Paul Atreides, and they'll help you. Feel free to replace the word "fear" with whatever stress you're facing at the moment, like dirty diapers. Sometimes parenting is like the infamous Gom Jabbar used as a deterrent in the pain test administered by the Bene Gesserit priestesses—a test to see which is stronger, instinct or awareness.

"I must not fear.
Fear is the mind-killer.
Fear is the little-death
that brings total obliteration.
I will face my fear.
I will permit it to pass over me and through me.
And when it has gone past
I will turn the inner eye to see its path.
Where the fear has gone
there will be nothing.
Only I will remain."

—FRANK HERBERT, *DUNE*

When your geekling is old enough, you can teach this mantra to him so he can use it when his parents (that's you) are lecturing him.

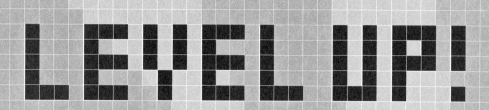

LEVEL UP!

Once again, it's time to count up experience points and see if your geekling has leveled up. This level is no joke; by now your geekling has a pretty good understanding of how the world works and how to interact with it. In short, things are getting awesome.

HEIGHT: _____ HAIR: _____

GEEKIEST MOMENT: _____

_____

FAVORITE TOY OR OBJECT: _____

_____

MOST ADVENTUROUS MOMENTS: _____

_____

FAVORITE THINGS TO SAY/TALK ABOUT: _____

_____

FAVORITE GEEK THINGS TO DO: _____

_____

SECOND BIRTHDAY

It's a birthday! It's time to celebrate all that hard work exploring the wide world and getting the hang of this whole "being human" thing. Send out some video–game themed invites, pick up some party hats that look like something a wizard would wear and prepare some games because it's time to party!

WHAT KIND OF CELEBRATION DID YOU HAVE FOR BABY'S SECOND BIRTHDAY?

- ☐ Party
- ☐ Dinner
- ☐ Murder mystery
- ☐ Other ....

PRESENTS RECEIVED: ....

....

....

....

....

WHO ATTENDED: ....

....

....

....

GAMES PLAYED: ....

....

BEST PART OF THE BIRTHDAY: ....

....

....

....

WORST PART OF THE BIRTHDAY: ....

....

....

TECHNOLOGY AND CHILD

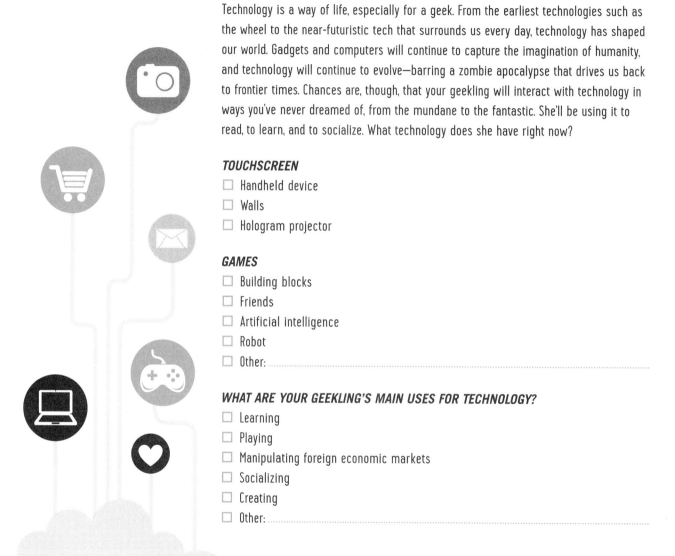

Technology is a way of life, especially for a geek. From the earliest technologies such as the wheel to the near-futuristic tech that surrounds us every day, technology has shaped our world. Gadgets and computers will continue to capture the imagination of humanity, and technology will continue to evolve—barring a zombie apocalypse that drives us back to frontier times. Chances are, though, that your geekling will interact with technology in ways you've never dreamed of, from the mundane to the fantastic. She'll be using it to read, to learn, and to socialize. What technology does she have right now?

TOUCHSCREEN
☐ Handheld device
☐ Walls
☐ Hologram projector

GAMES
☐ Building blocks
☐ Friends
☐ Artificial intelligence
☐ Robot
☐ Other: ....

WHAT ARE YOUR GEEKLING'S MAIN USES FOR TECHNOLOGY?
☐ Learning
☐ Playing
☐ Manipulating foreign economic markets
☐ Socializing
☐ Creating
☐ Other: ....

WORDS OF WISDOM

"We spend the first year of a child's life

teaching it to walk and talk and the rest

of its life to shut up and sit down.

There's something wrong there."

—NEIL DEGRASSE TYSON

Making It in a Science-Fiction Universe

By the time your geekling is old enough to actually want to read this, we'll be an indeterminate number of years in the future. The miraculous technology that we take for granted today will probably have evolved into something even more amazing—perhaps even seemingly magical. There is no way to predict how technology will advance, and you're already bringing your geekling into a highly technological world, but by the time they're grown it promises to be an all-out science fiction universe. How science fiction will your geekling's future be?

HOW DOES GEEKLING GET TO SCHOOL?

- ☐ Walking on a hovering walkway
- ☐ Flying electric car
- ☐ Teleportation
- ☐ Jetpack
- ☐ Doesn't; lessons are downloaded via brain implants
- ☐ Carried by personal robot assistant
- ☐ By armored bus/car to protect from the mutants
- ☐ Other

DOES GEEKLING'S CLONE SHARE THE SAME NAME?

DATE OF FIRST ENCOUNTER WITH A TIME TRAVELER:

/ /

DATE TIME TRAVELER CHANGED THE DATE OF FIRST ENCOUNTER:

/ /

NAME OF FIRST CONTACT ALIEN RACE:

FIRST TRIP INTO OUTER SPACE:

/ /

NAME OF FIRST PERSONAL ARTIFICIAL INTELLIGENCE:

DATE PERSONAL ARTIFICIAL INTELLIGENCE WENT ROGUE AND TOOK OVER THE WORLD:

/ /

WORDS OF WISDOM

"Children see magic because

they look for it."

—CHRISTOPHER MOORE,
LAMB: THE GOSPEL ACCORDING TO BIFF,
CHRIST'S CHILDHOOD PAL

BABY'S FIRST LOVECRAFT

It's never too early to teach your child about the malicious aloofness of the universe and about the frightening, nameless things that hover just on the edge of our vision. It would be a terrible thing for your child to walk blissfully through life, never truly understanding the awful, mind-breaking secrets of existence. The cosmos does not care, and the only gods that exist are alien things that dance and gibber mindlessly at the center of infinity and rend worlds asunder. Honestly, the best way to teach your geekling about the universe's malign indifference is to read those black, cramped passages scrawled on the pages of the dread *Necronomicon*. But who can afford one of those?

The second best way is to make certain that the kid gets comfortable with the idea of serving the mighty Cthulhu, because once the dead but dreaming priest of the Great Old Ones is liberated from his undersea tomb, the corpse city of R'lyeh, he will devour his worshipers last. Maybe. Start gaining favor with "that which is not-dead-but-dreaming" by purchasing one of the many plush dolls that have been made in homage to the mighty Cthulhu. Or, even better, follow the following instructions and make your own!

Create Your Own
Sock Cthulhu

You'll Need:

- ONE PACK OF GREEN DRESS SOCKS
- ONE PACKAGE OF COTTON BATTING OR COTTON BALLS
- GREEN OPAQUE PANTYHOSE

- ONE PACK OF GREEN RUBBER BANDS
- GLUE GUN
- ONE PACKAGE OF GOOGLY EYES

1. Take the socks out of the package. These will be Great Cthulhu's tentacles. Stuff them full of the cotton batting, leaving about an inch or so of empty space at the top. Set them aside.

2. Cut off about a six-inch piece of pantyhose leg. Make sure that you keep part of the closed foot end. Stuff the hose with cotton batting. Try to make it as round as possible to form the head, and leave a half-inch of empty space at the open end.

3. Bunch up the open ends of the socks and the hose, close each of them off with a rubber band, then use the rubber bands to join all of the tied ends together. Fit the sock "tentacles" as evenly as possible into the open end of the headpiece. Tie the whole thing closed with more rubber bands.

4. Using the glue gun, stick a few googly eyes onto the head piece. Don't be afraid to use a bunch, Mighty Cthulhu sees all anyway.

5. Chant the names of the Great Old Ones who live beneath the mountains, under the sweeping desert sands in the east, who cling to asteroids in deep space, and those who walk primal and unseen in dimensions overlapping ours. If you're lucky, the powers of Great Old Ones will infuse your Sock Cthulhu, shattering the placid island of ignorance on which you currently live.

6. Go mad.

Making It in the Post-Apocalyptic World

Geek culture has a long history of embracing post-apocalyptic scenarios. Mad Max's endless desert wasteland, the radiation-ravaged landscape of the Fallout series of video games, and *The Walking Dead*'s nihilistic zombie-infested afterworld make it seem as if society is always teetering on the edge of collapse. Mere anarchy is seconds away from our door. How will you and your geekling make it through the mutant-zombie-dinosaur-infested post-war world?

HOW DID THE WORLD END?

☐ With a bang
☐ With a whimper
☐ Zombies
☐ Evil artificial intelligence
☐ Other: ....

HOW DO YOU GET AROUND?

☐ Armored muscle car
☐ Armored jogging stroller
☐ Walking
☐ Other: ....

ZOMBIE KILLS: ....

MUTANT KILLS: ....

KILLS: ....

Sooner or later your geekling will have to leave the nest and go to daycare or preschool. It will be time for her to show off all of her geekeries to other children. She'll make other geek friends, and learn more about the world outside of the Fortress of Solitude. It will be a great adventure.

FIRST DAY AT SCHOOL—HOW DID IT GO?

....

....

....

HOW DIFFICULT WAS IT FOR YOUR GEEKLING TO SEPARATE FROM YOU?

....

....

FRIENDS MADE:

....

....

ENEMIES MADE:

....

....

COUPS ORGANIZED:

....

....

TEACHER

☐ Alien
☐ Robot
☐ Other...

FAVORITE PART OF THE DAY:

....

....

FAVORITE NEW THINGS LEARNED:

....

....

LEVEL UP!

Another year has passed and your geekling is kicking butt and taking names. If he's not already ruling the world, he's well on his way.

HEIGHT: _____ HAIR: _____

GEEKIEST MOMENT: _____

_____

FAVORITE SAYING: _____

_____

ADVENTUROUS MOMENTS: _____

_____

FAVORITE THINGS TO SAY/TALK ABOUT: _____

_____

FAVORITE GEEK THINGS TO DO: _____

_____

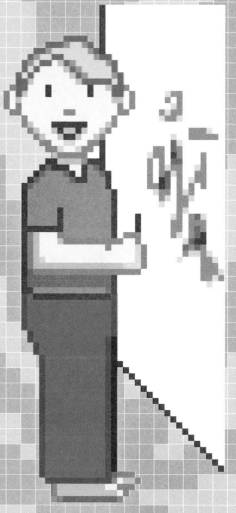

THIRD BIRTHDAY

Your geekling has spent the past year playing games, listening to stories, and developing her own geek passions and interests. Time to celebrate!

**WHAT KIND OF CELEBRATION DID YOU HAVE
FOR YOUR CHILD'S THIRD BIRTHDAY?**

☐ Party
☐ Dinner
☐ LAN Party
☐ Other

PRESENTS RECEIVED:

WHO ATTENDED:

GAMES PLAYED:

BEST PART OF THE BIRTHDAY:

WORST PART OF THE BIRTHDAY:

PETS, ANIMAL COMPANIONS, and FAMILIARS

There is a long tradition of heroes, wizards, and geeks who have had animal companions or familiars. Harry Potter had Hedwig the owl, Hermione had Crookshanks the cat, and even Han Solo had Chewbacca . . . that counts, right?

There's a strong chance that your geek family will have a dog or a cat—maybe even both—and there's nothing like seeing your geekling bond with an animal. Maybe she's bonded with a pet you already have, maybe she snuggles a pet you got after her arrival, or maybe your geekling has adopted an alien creature that's been stranded on earth. Whatever the case may be, sit back and enjoy the interactions and government conspiracies that you're sure to encounter due to your geekling's bond with her new companion.

FIRST KIND OF PET: ....

PET'S NAME: ....

FIRST TIME RIDDEN INTO BATTLE:

....

....

....

FIRST MAGICAL ANIMAL FAMILIAR:
- ☐ Owl
- ☐ Hawk
- ☐ Rat
- ☐ Cat
- ☐ Dog

HOW SUMMONED: ....

....

WORDS OF WISDOM

"Kids'll look up,

they won't look down."

—JOE RUBY,
THUNDARR THE BARBARIAN
AND *SCOOBY-DOO*

Making It in a Fantasy Universe

The truth is, no one really knows what will happen in the future. Once the world was filled with tales of elves and dragons. Accounts of faerie folk and magic swords have been with us since humans first sat around the fire, telling stories. You never know when the ancient forces of magic and the supernatural will once again emerge. Perhaps one day the world egg will crack and Jörmungandr, the Midgard Serpent, will release the earth and giants will once again stride like mountains. We want baby to be prepared for that, right?

FANTASY NAME: ....

(Use the chart Random Awesomeness Chart from earlier to generate one)

FIRST MAGIC ITEM:

☐ Ring of: ....

☐ Magic Sword of: ....

☐ Cloak of: ....

WHAT SKILL HAS YOUR CHILD LEARNED THAT WILL BE MOST USEFUL IN A FANTASY WORLD?

....

....

....

Craft a Magic Item

As any hero knows, making it in a fantasy universe takes not only courage, skill, and determination, but also magic. Magic items give champions the edge they need to make it through tough quests—like going to school or to the doctor's office. Magic items are usually found during the quest, but there's no reason your little geek can't create his own to aid in his journey. Here's how to create your own magic item:

1. Find an object that you can carry around easily. A coin works great, a bowling ball not so well.

2. Create a rune of power. To do this, write a sentence that describes the power you would like to have bestowed upon you whenever you activate your item. You can charge your item to enhance your courage, your intelligence, or your creativity. For instance:

   + I have the courage of a tiger.
   + I am the smartest kid in the class.
   + I have the power to become invisible.

3. Now take all of the letters in your sentence and jumble them together. You can drop repeating letters or vowels to give yourself just a few letters to work with. You want to create a single "rune" that absorbs the meaning of the sentence.

4. Design the rune by drawing the letters together. They can overlap, rotate, or anything you want to do that makes them look cool and magical.

5. When you have designed your rune, draw it on your object. As you do this, chant sorcerous rhymes.

6. Decide how to activate the item. How do you release its power? Maybe you have to touch it. Maybe you have to say a specific word or phrase. Once you decide that, your magic item is charged and ready to use! Use it whenever you need a boost to your courage or need to turn invisible. Results may vary. The author and the publisher of this book do not guarantee results. If you feel like your object is running out of power, feel free to make a new one.

LEVEL UP!

For four years your geek has been exploring the world around her, learning about you and herself, having all manner of exciting experiences, as well as bad days and good days. Your geekling is growing, changing, becoming more and more her own person. Let's continue to chart her growth.

HEIGHT: _____ *HAIR:* _____

GEEKIEST MOMENT: _____

_____

FAVORITE THINGS TO DO:

_____

_____

_____

_____

BEST THING TO HAPPEN THIS YEAR:

_____

_____

_____

FOURTH BIRTHDAY

Four years old! Your little geek is counting and talking and playing games. This is where you really get to party hearty. Break out a board game, take the cake out of the oven, and distribute the juice boxes, because it's time to celebrate!

WHAT KIND OF CELEBRATION DID YOU HAVE FOR YOUR GEEKLING'S FOURTH BIRTHDAY?

☐ Party

☐ Dinner

☐ Masquerade

☐ Other

PRESENTS RECEIVED:

WHO ATTENDED:

GAMES PLAYED:

BEST PART OF THE BIRTHDAY:

WORST PART OF THE BIRTHDAY:

ROLE-PLAYING GAMES

There's nothing else that's quite like a tabletop pen-and-paper role-playing game. Role-playing games (RPGs) are truly interactive entertainment where all players are in control of the story and everyone has the chance to shine. Many a geek has cut his teeth on role-playing games and has learned the basics of mathematics, social interaction, and storytelling, all while having fun. Many of those geeks have taken those lessons into the real world and become successful actors, directors, comedians, and business people. It'll be a while before your geekling is ready to tackle a full-on role-playing game, but when it happens, record those first special moments here:

FIRST CHARACTER:

FIRST CHARACTER DEATH:

FIRST MODULE PLAYED:

FIRST CREATURE ENCOUNTER:

FIRST TRAP SPRUNG:

FIRST TRAP DISABLED:

While you're waiting for your geekling to get to the right age to play an RPG, you can get him ready by introducing the concepts of adventuring for gold and glory. Hide treasure around the house—things like coins or costume jewelry. Create a treasure map he can use to find the cache, and place obstacles he needs to overcome in order to win the treasure. Drape a sheet over yourself and play dangerous creatures and gelatinous guardians that your child will need to fight, sneak past, or overcome.

GEEKLING THE VAMPIRE SLAYER

By now your geekling should be showing some propensity towards a specific skill or interest. Maybe she's a little storyteller, or maybe she's good at basic math, drawing and coloring, or building things with blocks or Legos. The things that she's interested in now might give you an idea about what she might be good at when she's a full-grown adult geek.

THINGS GEEKLING IS GOOD AT: ....

....

THINGS GEEKLING IS NOT SO GOOD AT: ....

....

GEEKLING HAS THE MOST FUN DOING: ....

....

GEEKLING HATES DOING: ....

....

WHEN LITTLE GEEK GROWS UP, SHE WANTS TO BE (check all that apply):

- ☐ Superhero
- ☐ Vampire slayer
- ☐ Consulting detective
- ☐ Lawyer
- ☐ Doctor
- ☐ Space explorer
- ☐ Mercenary
- ☐ Pony
- ☐ Wizard
- ☐ Writer
- ☐ Artist
- ☐ Scientist
- ☐ Cyborg
- ☐ Engineer
- ☐ Vampire
- ☐ Archaeologist (real)
- ☐ Archaeologist (like Indiana Jones)

WHEN LITTLE GEEK GROWS UP, PARENT WANTS HER TO BE (check all that apply):

- ☐ Superhero
- ☐ Vampire slayer
- ☐ Consulting detective
- ☐ Lawyer
- ☐ Doctor
- ☐ Space explorer
- ☐ Mercenary
- ☐ Pony
- ☐ Wizard
- ☐ Writer
- ☐ Artist
- ☐ Scientist
- ☐ Cyborg
- ☐ Engineer
- ☐ Vampire
- ☐ Archaeologist (real)
- ☐ Archaeologist (like Indiana Jones)

LEVEL UP!

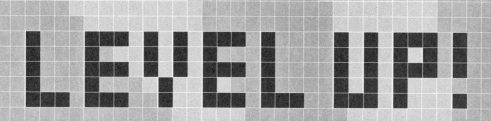

Five years old! Your little geek is practically a person now. He's old enough to do simple math, and to tell stories. He's probably old enough to start playing a simple role-playing game. All that hard work is paying off; let's see how much your geekling has grown.

HEIGHT: _____ HAIR: _____

GEEKIEST MOMENT: _____

_____

FAVORITE THING: _____

_____

LEAST FAVORITE THING: _____

_____

SAYINGS OR CATCHPHRASES: _____

FAVORITE BOOK: _____

FAVORITE TV SHOW: _____

FAVORITE MOVIE: _____

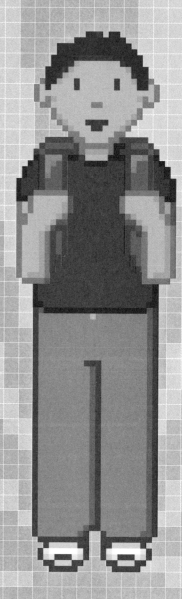

FIFTH BIRTHDAY

Five years old! This is a big one. Your geekling has been through a lot, has conquered many skills, and seen a lot of what the world has to offer—yet things will still be magical and wondrous for her. Celebrate all of her hard work by doing something super fun on her birthday.

WHAT KIND OF CELEBRATION DID YOU HAVE FOR YOUR GEEKLING'S FIFTH BIRTHDAY?

☐ Party
☐ Dinner
☐ Séance
☐ Other ....

PRESENTS RECEIVED: ....

....

....

....

WHO ATTENDED: ....

....

....

....

GAMES PLAYED: ....

....

BEST PART OF THE BIRTHDAY: ....

....

....

WORST PART OF THE BIRTHDAY: ....

....

....

WORDS OF WISDOM

"Most things are good, and they are the strongest things; but there are evil things too, and you are not doing a child a favor by trying to shield him from reality. The important thing is to teach a child that good can always triumph over evil."

—WALT DISNEY